Infections of

A

Sad Mind

Introduction

When I went to college and realized I enjoyed writing, I didn't want to believe it. In all honesty, I'm an asshole who has a mushy side. When it comes to writing, my heart likes to finally come out as if I am a 1950's housewife in therapy. You will see in these poems, for once in my life, my true emotions. Reader you will discover things not even my mother knows. Things that may make you regret. It will be a journey where you can repeat back to a certain time on your life, and ponder on it. From the bottom of my gut I hope you enjoy my book.

There is no shame in remembering things, but my only advice I can give you is...

Perhaps, move on.

To every
infected mind.

Table of Contants

Give Me Sanity

Dull

February

Toxic

Hey Doc

Eye Catcher

Come Closer

Guess This Is Goodbye

Thrift

Garbage

Rebirth

Infected Mind

Devil Dancing

She had the prettiest high eyes
and the loveliest hair
her eyes were green with a touch of yellow
like dry grass but you still lay on it
she wore her hair however she pleased
and it was breathtaking each time
as if angels came down
each day and combed it themselves
I beloved this girl
still
she left
I never got to say these words to her
thus the bitter stale artist
steps away
and lets these lines dance inside her head.

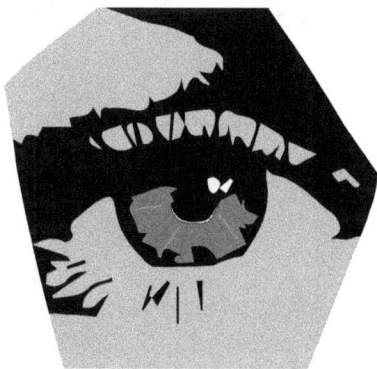

NE > MN > NE

Even With my empty green eyes, messy hair, and a scar on my lip.

I still felt vital.

Almost as if I was part of some painstaking plan.

Like it was meant to be.

I'm here.
And I'm alive.

Fazed

I never escort away the option
to be sad.
I am in an evil love affair with depression
and sad love songs.
I will always find ways to think of you
just so I can drive in silence
and mumble all the words I prayed
I could have said to you.

Quiet frankly
it's better
sleeping alone

Useless Gardens

I'm a hopeless romantic
trying to grow roses
for the girl who will never want them

Parallel

I have these pictures I show myself in my
head.
They are not real pictures.
They are not even real moments.
They are in fact these parallel universes
created in my brain where you and I are
together.

In the end I am here in this universe alone.

Without you

apt. 251

I came over to your place.
It smelled clean and your washer and
dryer had musical beat to them.
You were napping and breathing slow.
You looked sweet curled up with a grin
on your face.
I wanted to crawl in bed with you.
But you had only just met me.

Car Radios

Sitting in a car without the radio playing
is so odd to me.
I feel so uncomfortable and unsettled.
I need the background noise.
Growing up my parents would never play the radio
and it drove me mad.
I didn't understand how two individuals could sit in
such fucking silence and not feel like something is off.
Its idiotic.
But in all reality my parents probably just forgot to
turn the radio on.

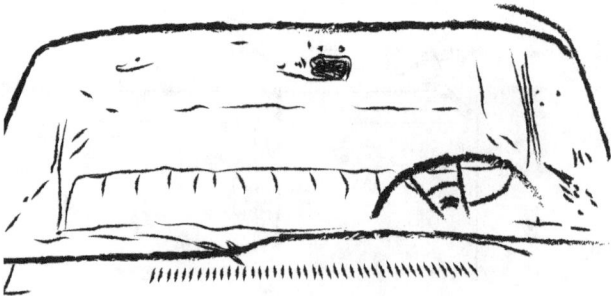

Only

I think the only thing
I could ever want
in my life
would have to be
for all my loved ones
to just be happy.

Mindlessly happy.

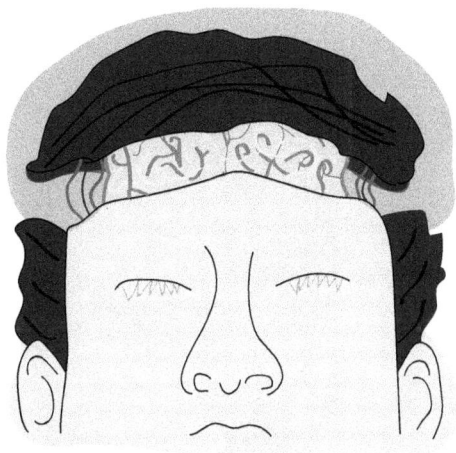

Drops

Perhaps if when it rained
and every rain drop
were a diamond
people would stop marrying
the wrong people.

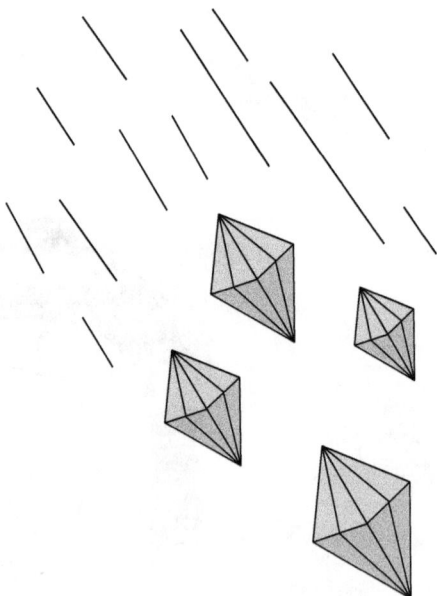

Pipe dream

She is a
scary, disturbed, miserable
pipe dream
that I can not
stop thinking about.

Bad Breath

The taste of your cigarettes
remains on my lips
the rest of the night.
Even when I wake
with a hangover
you're all I taste.

Wreckage

I want to make
terrible, horrible, no good
decisions with you
forever and ever.

Hereafter

You never loved me
you only held my hands when it was winter
the water under the bridge is cold
but your heart was colder
the last thing I remember
after it all turned to dust
is being passed out on the floor
looking up
overjoyed I dumped you.

Let Me Tell You

I know many confessions
that people hold tender
they spew them out anywhere
as if I was a priest
in dumpy bar bathrooms, on the back of truck beds,
4 beers deep I can say these words to you because it's
a class reunion confessions
nevertheless I'm dazed
what do I do with these confessions
I guess I'll just let them eat me away

gradually

Pour

Let me see
how fucked up you are
so we can be fucked up

t o g e t h e r .

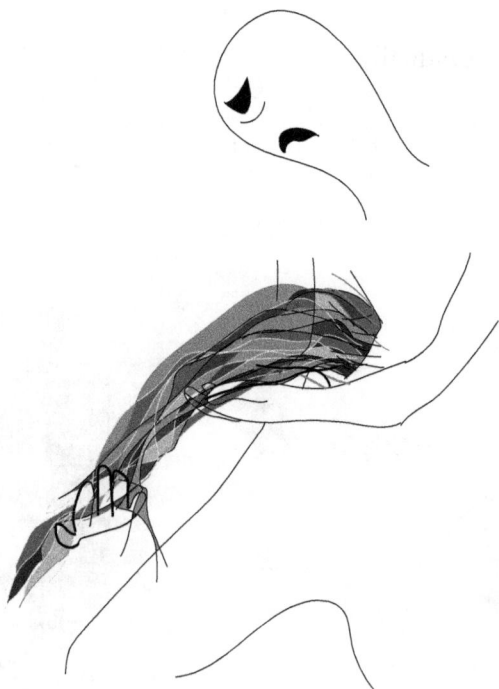

Kissed

Raindrops fell into my coffee
as if Mother Nature
wanted to touch my lips
and say good morning.

Idiot

I'm pretty bad with
irrational quetions
I always want to answer

Why the hell did you even ask?

New Era Girl

She had an aesthetic
that I truly could not fathom
I stayed up gazing at her
at long last
it was worth it
just to see her move the hair
from her eyes

Ground

I was high
trying to get cigerettes
then suddenly
the store got robbed.

Empty Cup

I was standing in a crowd
at a house party
starring off into space
and in that moment
I realized, I don't love you
you are nothing
but a fascination I had
when I was alone and yearning.

Home Body

I hurl my lucky cigerette
into the abyss of my empy beer bottle
I begin to hear spuzzling
not from the butt
it came from the sorry excuse
of a get-together inside
the pack of goons who are hosting
are filth
I dont have time for this

I'm going home.

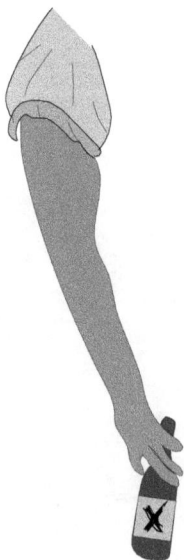

Nebraskan

You will always belong to this state
what you've done.
pastures you've loved
how you were raised.
she is your home
she might really fucking suck
however you damn well adore her
we are her keeper.
this is where I will be buried
Nebraska you are my final
resting place.

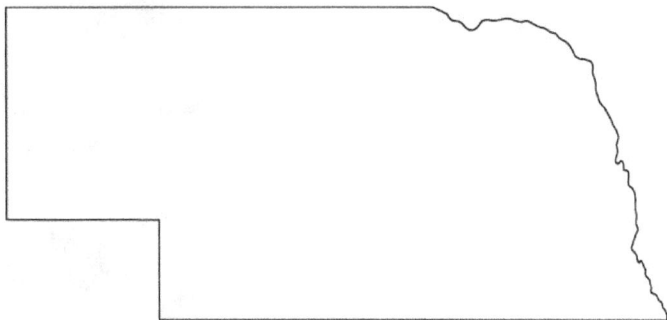

Apt. 12

Day by day I have grown to love you
you broke down more times than
matinance could fix
I still would come home to you.
Walking into this nook
felt like boarding mothership
you got to shed your skin
and crawl around a bit
this place has never been evil
never been cruel
she did her best
and kept us safe
shes is my sweat, tears, and sorrows
but she saw the becomings
of liberated souls.

Catholics

She gets more upset
about eating meat
on a friday
than fucking me
when she has a boyfriend.

Heartbeats

The girl I marry. The women I give my life to
is going to have to be one bad ass female.
She is going to have to put up
with so much bullshit.
She will be strong and patient.
I am a walking, talking nightmare.
I can hardly get myself to find reason
why I should even be here.
She will witness so much agony and turmoil
but I swear to whoever is our creator
I will love this woman
she will never experience a day in her life
where I am not there to be
her anything.

Therapy

I wake up in the morning
I look into your pastel eyes
this depression is getting
the best of me
you whisper your sweet nothings

Lipstick

I love when I see a cigarette butt
with lipstick on it
I always like to vision
what bad bitch
came outside
took some drags
then proceded to walk inside
and rip hearts out.

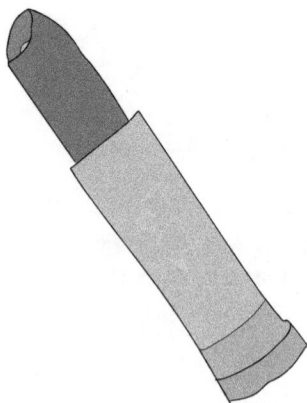

Touchy Feely

I keep having these dreams
of people touching
their loved ones back
I think it could be perhaps
that when you touch
someones back
its comfort
its love
and thats all
I desire.

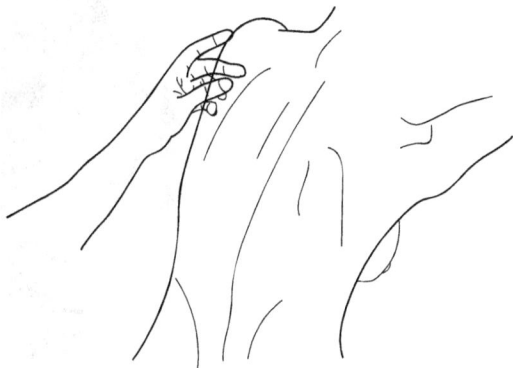

Punk

You're wasting
your time
not taking every chance
you get
to raise complete chaos.

The Worst

You put the most
SOUR fucking taste
in my mouth
it burns my cheeks
and fills them with acid

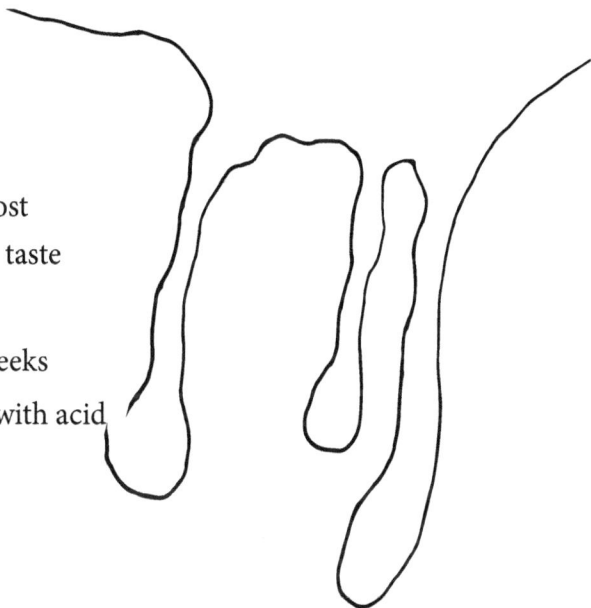

Mornings

I pace in the kitchen
everyday
fixing myself
as well as all the things
around me
planing my day
trying to get ahold of myself

*But for the love of god
I can not calm down.*

No trespassing

I will avoid you
with all my will
I refuse to let you
put a hold on me
every second

is *hell*

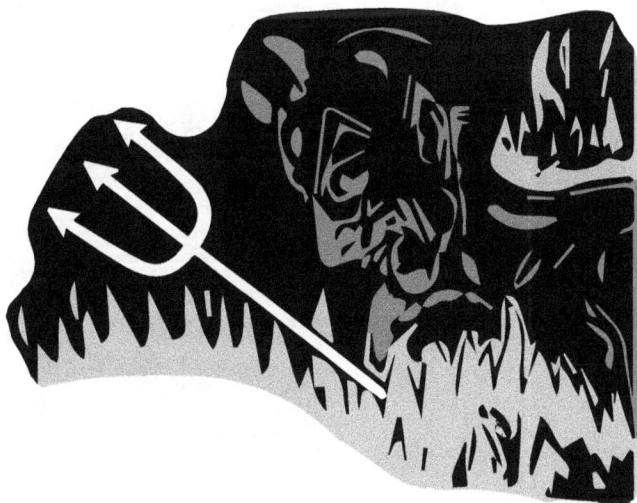

Under the Influence

One bottle, two bottle, three bottle,
four.
Five bottle, six bottle,
seven.
I'm drunk again.

Shuffleing around our block
wishing you'd call me
home.

For me

I don't know who's up there
but I will say this to you
I want to be better

I will be better.

Zoe

We see the truth in people
you and I
I think that's why
I enjoy you
you have no time
for bullshit
and neither do I.

Old Timer

"It's raining
like a cow
pissing
on a flat rock."

-My Father

Transform

I lose myself
and I always become
a part of you
I wish I could stay me

however I always
morph into you

Banal

Relationships are tedious
it's basically
just two people
renting eachothers
genitals.

She asked me to
write her a poem

yet I have already written her
thousands.

First Day

I didn't believe in love
at first sight
until I saw you
in your yellow cardigan
along with a striped shirt
I saw doubles when I looked at you
as if time slowed
I don't remember walking up to you
but before I knew it
you were looking up at me
and smiling
that's when I knew
I was yours
and nobody elses.

Disbelief

You kissed my scars
you know how I got them
you've seen the pain
these wounds give me
you still think
I'm beautiful
this love can not be real
no one could ever love me this way
I am broken
I am useless
I am nothing.

Artifact

I will tell her
every single truth
about myself
if she loves me
she will accept these facts
and still believe I'm worth
ivory and gold

Goth

I want to walk
into a dark forest
and spend eternity
with your ghost

Dull

I used to want
to set the world on fire

but now I want to watch
the world kill itself.

February

Half put aways dishes
burnt out light bulbs
and countless drifting thoughts
as well as daydreams.
It is inaccessible
to get anything done
when she is on my conscious.

Lynn

Whenever her time comes
I hope her spirit
becomes a planet
that is sustainable of life

that way she could be a mother
for all.

The Club

It was dark
my brother and I were stoned
he babbles on about how
gorrillas know their birthdays
but I was just happy to be content
the room is aluminated
with orange and blues
its better here
its nirvana

Time Travelers Wife

I love a good time travel conspiracy.
You know the ones where you see a person
from the future in a picture from the past.
I want to believe they are true.
If I was offered to see my life 10 years from
now.
I would go.
I would only want a glimpse.
To see if life is worth living.
Or worth dying.
Either way I would always live with
the unbearable sorrow of knowing how my
other life could have been.

You've Moved On

I walked past you
I could smell your scent
it brought me back to a time
when I thought I had a chance with you
I realize now that you and I
will never be
I cant stop thinking about you
but it's best for me to just
let you go.

Toxic

You will never find
your person
if you willingly

stay

while knowing they aren't the one.

Respect yourself enough
to be single.

Respect yourself enough
to let love find you.

Hey Doc

Once you get prescribed
pills
for your mental illness
you're glad
however you hate it
they fuck with your brain
making you emotionless
making your life shift.

If only I didn't want to die.
I wouldn't have to take these pills

Eye Catcher

You have lost your pigment
but none of your beauty.
A truly sublime mutation
it has become somewhat
of a weakness
of mine
that is impossible to resist.

She is a flower
of mixed petals
I must pick.

Come Closer

If I stay away from you
it's bullshit.

Every moment
that passes
I'm regreting.

Please know
every part of me
wants to embrace you.

Guess This Is Goodbye

Goodbye my love.
I am here physically
you can smell me
touch me
hear the sound of my voice.

Spiritually however
I've been gone
for months.

I don't feel
see
or want anymore

I have vansished.

There is no possible way
I could come back
from this.

Thrift

Take me to
a secondhand store
where I observe
you admiring
the antiques

while I bury
my face
into your neck

as you are
asorbing the aroma
of the eldery elements
around you.

Garbage

We do a lot for luck.
Amputating rabbits feet.
Praying on the number 7
Homicide of a black cat.
Still I must tell you
it's a lie.
Our world doesn't
give it to you
unless you steal it.

Rebirth

I once didn't cry
For 8 whole months
I thought this
Was the method
To my madness
I shoved everything
Into the depths of my heart
And left it there
It was absolute torture

I was to tough
For too long

So please
Let that shit out

Cleanse yourself of your burdens.

Infected Mind

You may lie awake
Staring into the black
Of your ceiling
Wondering
when will the sadness end

that day will come
you will know because

You will no longer
Lie awake aching

Only distracted
By them.

www.ingramcontent.com/pod-product-compliance
Lightning Source LLC
Chambersburg PA
CBHW060536030426
42337CB00021B/4283